אב
Bo

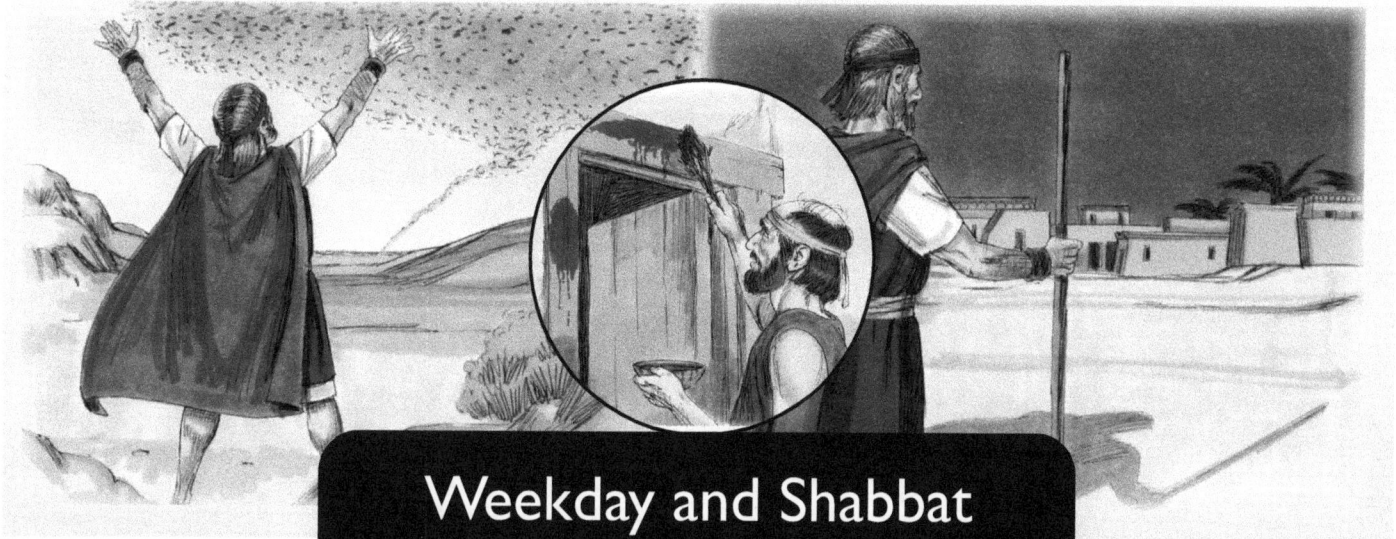

Weekday and Shabbat Afternoon Edition

Elliott Michaelson
MAJS

Copyright Information

PARASHAT BO

Vital Statistics	
Full text reference:	*Shemot / Exodus* 10: 1 to 13: 16
First Aliyah:	*Shemot / Exodus* 10: 1-3
Second Aliyah:	*Shemot / Exodus* 10: 4-6
Third Aliyah:	*Shemot / Exodus* 10: 7-11

Note: the English retelling of the Torah is for the entire parashah, not just the Shabbat pm / Weekday readings. The English for these readings consists of the first part of the retelling.

MY PROGRESS

Date	Torah blessings	Torah reading	Torah review in English

Date	Torah blessings	Torah reading	Torah review in English

Date	Torah blessings	Torah reading	Torah review in English

Date	Torah blessings	Torah reading	Torah review in English

BEFORE YOU BEGIN: GOOD THINGS TO ASK ABOUT THIS BOOK

Welcome to your Bar/Bat Mitzvah Survival Guide! There are some unique features about this guide that might be useful to you during your studies, such as...

What's up with the names of people and places?

Brace yourself, for what I'm about to say (or write, actually) may come as a shock. THE TORAH IS WRITTEN IN HEBREW. Big surprise, I know. So here's the issue many of my students have: in English, we call him *Moses* but in the Torah, we call him *Moshe*. The first woman on Earth is called *Eve* but in Hebrew, she's called *Hava*. The Jews were slaves in *Egypt* — or was it *Mitzra'im*? The answer is both. To try to avoid this confusion between English and Hebrew names, I've decided to stick with the Hebrew. So מֹשֶׁה is translated as *Moshe*, not *Moses*, and יְרוּשָׁלַיִם is *Yerushalayim*, not *Jerusalem*. For more on how to pronounce the Hebrew names, check out the handy translation chart on page ten.

How do you show God talking?

Many of us think of God as an inspirational force in our lives, but how many of us have actual physical conversations with God? As a kid, I was always confused by the fact that God physically speaks to people in the Torah but not to us today. When the Torah records God's "speech", we don't have to think of it as physical words all the time. Moses Maimonides was one of the greatest philosophers and teachers in Judaism, and 800 years ago he famously taught that all divine language in the Torah is metaphorical. Taking that to heart, I've done my very best to express that in my English retellings. God's "dialogue" is written in a different font and with a different tone, and I avoid using direct language like "said" or "told". So did Avraham hear the actual voice of God, or did God act as Avraham's inspirational inner voice? Both beliefs are valid, and it's something I encourage you to explore with your family and your teacher / rabbi.

In these retellings, I refer to God by two proper nouns: *Adonai* and *Elohim*. *Adonai* is God's actual, personal name: יְ-ה-ו-ה. You'll find it all over the place in the Tanah and in many sidurim. *Elohim* (אֱלֹהִים) is the Hebrew word for "God". Since the Tanah uses both as personal names for God, I've decided to keep the proper Hebrew terms.

What about commentary and translation?

Judaism has always accepted that the Torah text contains four layers of understanding. There's the literal, basic text that you see in front of you (peshat), but underneath the basic text are three layers of metaphorical understanding just waiting to be discovered (derash, remez, sod). You have over two thousand years of scholarship and commentary — including some great stuff being written today — to help you discover these hidden meanings. I've deliberately avoided providing them here for one all-important reason: any commentaries I select would reflect *my* perspective on the text and how it should be taught, and I want you to be free to find *your own way*. That's why I'm leaving the selection of commentary up to you and your rabbi / teacher.

Instead, I've devoted my time to a careful retelling of the Torah and Haftarah texts in English. This isn't a strict translation, but it isn't a sanitized children's version, either. My aim is to provide an English format that flows as easily as a work of juvenile literature, but which preserves the content and significance of the Biblical text. I've also included suggestions for study and analysis that are based on media literacy expectations from public school programs. These blurbs usually address social and historical questions that my own students ask because they need help understanding the ancient society that produced our sacred texts. None of this replaces Rabbinic commentary, but first you need to understand a little bit about the world of our ancient cousins. Then you can work with your rabbi / teacher to find the commentaries that speak to your own interests and concerns.

Da Links!

If you're using the ebook version of this book, try tapping the hyperlinks that appear periodically in the text. Some of them will take you to useful Google maps of many of the locations mentioned in the Torah, while others will take you the *Jewish Virtual Library* or *My Jewish Learning* to learn more about the famous people and nations from the Torah and Haftarah. Enjoy!

-- EM, fall 2015

TRANSLITERATIONS OF HEBREW VOWEL SOUNDS

(A very handy reference guide...)

E

Same sound as:
SPECIAL
THEM
HEAD

** Note that the *Shva* can also indicate the absence of a vowel sound.*

O

Same sound as:
HOPE
GROW
BOAT

A

Same sound as:
CUP
TROUBLE
SUPPER

U

Same sound as:
NOODLES
GROUP
SUPER

I

Same sound as:
MEATBALL
PIECE
AGREE

AY

Same sound as:
THEY
AGENT
STEAK

** Some pronounce the *Tzayreh* as "E", some pronounce it as "AY", and some use both pronunciations.*

AI

Same sound as:
EYEBALL
RIGHT
LIBRARY

Our *Bar/Bat Mitzvah Survival Guides* use the proper Hebrew names for people and places. The transliterations on this page will help you pronounce them properly. Sometimes, the English and Hebrew names are very close, but often they're quite different. Here are some of the most common differences.

Ashur	Assyria
Bavel	Babylon
Mitzra'im	Egypt
Moshe	Moses
Rivkah	Rebekah
Sha'ul	Saul
Shlomo	Solomon
Ya'akov	Jacob
Yehezk'el	Ezekiel
Yehoshu'a	Joshua
Yehudah	Judah
Yerushalayim	Jerusalem
Yirmiyahu	Jeremiah
Yish'ayah	Isaiah
Yisra'el	Israel
Yitzhak	Isaac
Yosef	Joseph

PUTTING ON THE TALLIT & TEFILLIN

If you've never had the chance to put on the *tallit* or *tefillin*, this is your lucky day! Traditionally, the *tallit* and *tefillin* are worn for all weekday morning services. On Shabbat and Holy Day mornings, only the *tallit* is worn (except Yom Kippur, when we wear the tallit all day). Why the difference? There are many explanations. My favorite reason goes like this: the Torah teaches us to wear reminders of our Divine Agreement with God on our arms and our heads (i.e. *tefillin*). On Shabbat, Pesah, Shavu'ot, Sukkot, Rosh Hashanah, and Yom Kippur, we perform rituals all day long that remind us of God's Agreement with us, so we don't need the *tefillin* to remind us. To put everything on, follow these basic steps. You can also find a video on our website at **http://www.adventurejudaism.net/Bar_Bat_Mitzvah_Guides.html**.

1 Recite the brahah for wrapping yourself in the tallit.

בָּרוּךְ אַתָּה יְיָ אֱלֹהֵינוּ מֶלֶךְ הָעוֹלָם, אֲשֶׁר קִדְּשָׁנוּ בְּמִצְוֹתָיו, וְצִוָּנוּ לְהִתְעַטֵּף בַּצִּיצִת.

We praise You, Adonai our God, Ruler of the universe, whose *mitzvot* make us holy, and who commanded us to cover ourselves with *tzitzit*.

2 Wrap the collar around your shoulders as if you were putting on a cape.

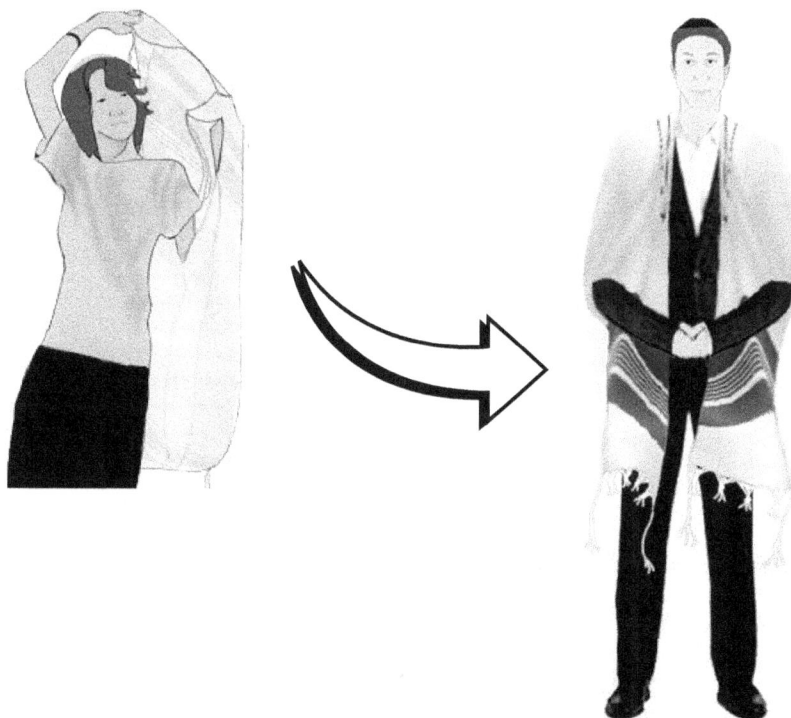

On Shabbat and Holy Day mornings, stop here!

3 Loop the *tefillin shel yad* (the one with the extra-long strap) around your bicep.

If you're left-handed, use your right bicep. If you're right-handed, use your left bicep. If you're ambidextrous like me, take your pick!

4 Before tightening the loop, recite this brahah.

בָּרוּךְ אַתָּה יְיָ אֱלֹהֵינוּ מֶלֶךְ הָעוֹלָם, אֲשֶׁר קִדְּשָׁנוּ בְּמִצְוֹתָיו, וְצִוָּנוּ לְהָנִיחַ תְּפִלִּין.

We praise You, Adonai our God, Ruler of the universe, whose *mitzvot* make us holy, and who commanded us to put on *tefillin*.

5 Tighten the loop around your bicep and wrap the strap around your forearm 7 times.

Wrap the strap around your forearm 7 times.

If the strap is long enough, use the extra length to keep the *tefillin* box in place on your bicep.

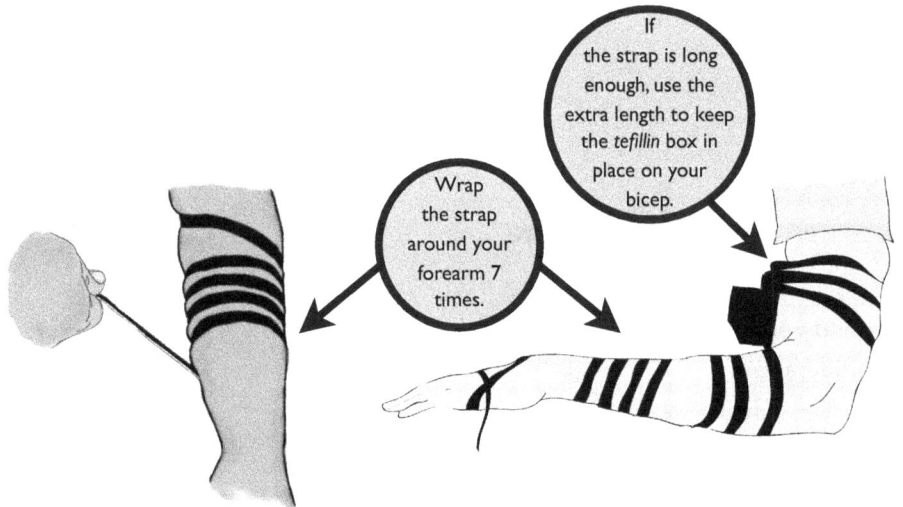

6 Place the *tefillin shel rosh* at the center of your forehead, right at the hairline.

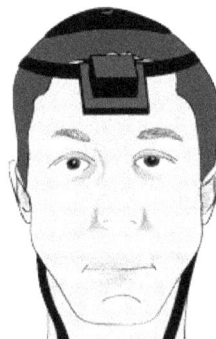

Two long straps extend from the back of the *tefillin shel rosh*. Let them hang freely on either side of your head.

7

Recite the bra<u>h</u>ah for the *tefillin shel rosh*.

בָּרוּךְ אַתָּה יְיָ אֱלֹהֵינוּ מֶלֶךְ הָעוֹלָם, אֲשֶׁר
קִדְּשָׁנוּ בְּמִצְוֹתָיו, וְצִוָּנוּ עַל מִצְוַת תְּפִלִּין.

We praise You, Adonai our God, Ruler of the universe,
whose *mitzvot* make us holy, and who commanded
the *mitzvah* of tefillin.

8

Finish wrapping the *tefillin shel yad* by winding it around your middle finger 3 times.

If the strap is long enough, you can also wind it around your hand to help keep everything in place.

Tefillin shel rosh with the two hanging straps.

Tefillin shel yad around the bicep (under the tallit.)

Tefillin shel yad wrapped 3 times around the middle finger.

Tefillin shel yad wrapped 7 times around the forearm.

You're ready to go! When you're finished, take everything off in the reverse order.

TORAH IN ENGLISH

SHEMOT / EXODUS 10: 1 TO 13: 16

What's the story so far?

It's been three generations since the final events of the book of *Bereshit / Genesis*. The family that began with Avraham & Sarah, Yitzhak & Rivkah, and the twelve sons of Ya'akov, Le'ah & Rahel, has now grown into the twelve tribes of Benay Yisra'el. A new king has taken over Mitzra'im (Egypt) who doesn't recognize the contributions of Ya'akov or his children. Fearing their power, this new Pharaoh has enslaved all of Benay Yisra'el to prevent them from becoming too numerous. But salvation is on the way: God has appointed a new leader, Moshe, to lead Benay Yisra'el to freedom. But first, a show of strength is needed in the form of miraculous plagues. As our parashah begins, Mitzra'im has already endured seven plagues. But the last three are yet to come...

What to expect in this parashah...

The first four *parashot* of *Shemot / Exodus* form one big story. *Parashat Bo* is the third in this series. The story relates of the enslavement of Benay Yisra'el and their rescue from Mitzra'im. This means that in order to fully understand what's going on in *Bo*, you need to read the first twelve chapters of *Shemot / Exodus*.

Aside from this, the Torah has several primary concerns that are reflected in this parashah:

(1) The Torah is interested in revealing the origins of the people of Israel;

(2) The Torah is interested in demonstrating God's power;

(3) The Torah wants to highlight God's special interest in the Jewish people and explain why the Jewish people have a special interest in God.

And so, without further ado, on to the Torah...

LOCUSTS LOCUSTS EVERYWHERE

10: 1-6
The Weekday & Shabbat
afternoon reading starts here.

Adonai's Presence came to Moshe.

I have hardened Par'oh's heart to demonstrate My power. You will tell the story of everything I have done in Mitzra'im to your children and your children's children, and you will realize that I am Adonai.

So Moshe and Aharon went to Par'oh to relate God's message.

"This is what Adonai, God of the Hebrew people, says: 'How much longer will you refuse to show humility in My presence? Send My people out so they can worship Me! If you do not let them

> **Hail:** Remember that this parashah is the middle part of a longer story arc in the Torah. For details on the first seven plagues, see *parashat Va-Era* (*Shemot / Exodus* chapters 7 to 9).

go, I will bring locusts across your borders tomorrow. The swarm will be so thick that you will be unable to see the ground! They will devour everything that survived the **hail** and eat every tree in your fields! They will fill the homes of all your servants — every home in Mitzra'im! It will be a swarm unlike anything your ancestors or their ancestors ever saw, unlike anything seen on Earth to this day!'"

With that, they left Par'oh's throne room.

10: 7-11
Weekday & Shabbat afternoon
reading ends at verse 11.

"How much longer will we let them trap us?" demanded Par'oh's courtiers after Moshe and Aharon were gone. "Let their men go and worship Adonai! Can't you see that Mitzra'im has lost?"

Par'oh gave in. He summoned Moshe and Aharon back into the chamber.

"Go and worship Adonai your God," he told them. "Who will go?"

"All of us," replied Moshe. "Our young and old, sons and daughters, even our flocks and herds. It's the time for Adonai's festival."

Par'oh shook his head and scoffed. "Send you *and* your children? Adonai must really be with you! But I see right through your trick! Your *men* can go to worship Adonai, since that is what you originally asked for!"

Par'oh motioned to his guards. "Get them out of my sight!"

Moshe and Aharon were tossed out of the room.

10: 12-15

Adonai's Presence came to Moshe again.

Extend your arm and sweep your hand across your view of Mitzra'im. Bring out the locusts to devour the vegetation and everything left over from the hail!

Moshe did so. Holding his staff, he extended his arm and swept it across the horizon. Adonai caused an eastern wind to blow all day and night, and when morning came, the **locusts** blew in. It was a plague unlike anything Mitzra'im had ever experienced; they infested the entire land. They covered so much of the ground that the land itself darkened. They ate all the vegetation and the fruit off of all the trees so that no plant remained untouched in all of Mitzra'im.

Locusts: I know it sounds gross, but swarms of locusts are actually common in this part of the world, even today. The Torah's description of how these swarms move around (blown by wind) and the way they devour everything is quite accurate. What's unique here is the magnitude of the plague. Locust swarms were (and still are) local disasters, not national ones. The Torah is depicting every farmer's (and every king's) worst nightmare.

Reed Sea: No, this isn't a typo. Everything you may have heard about the "Red Sea" is incorrect. No-one is exactly sure precisely where the ancient יַם סוּף was, but the Torah places it in the marshy region between the Gulf of Suez and the eastern end of the Nile Delta. In other words, somewhere along the course of the Suez Canal — <u>not</u> the Red Sea.

10: 16-20

Par'oh quickly summoned Moshe and Aharon.

"I have committed a great insult to Adonai your God and to you," admitted Par'oh. "Please forgive me just this once and beg Adonai your God on my behalf to remove this destruction from me!"

Moshe left Par'oh and begged Adonai on Par'oh's behalf. Adonai caused a westerly wind to carry the locusts into the **Reed Sea** so that not a single locust remained within Mitzra'im's borders. But Adonai caused Par'oh's heart to harden again, and he refused to let **Benay Yisra'el** go.

Benay Yisra'el: בְּנֵי יִשְׂרָאֵל literally means "children/descendants of Yisra'el". Yisra'el was the nickname that was given to Ya'akov after his world-famous wrestling match with God's servant (for details, see chapter 32 of *parashat Va-Yishlaḥ* in the book of *Bereshit*). Benay Yisra'el refers to the tribes who descended from Ya'akov's twelve sons. Since the Torah uses בְּנֵי יִשְׂרָאֵל as the proper name for these people, I've decided to keep it as a proper name in the English.

INTO DARKNESS

10:21-29

Adonai's Presence came to Moshe again.

Extend your hand up to the heavens to bring a thick, oppressive darkness over the land of
Mitzra'im.

Moshe did so, and a darkness fell on Mitzra'im that was so thick and oppressive that the people couldn't see each another. For three days, they stayed in their homes, unable to leave. But Benay Yisra'el had light in their homes.

Par'oh summoned Moshe.

"Leave, all of you! Worship Adonai! But your flocks and herds stay here," demanded Par'oh.

"You have to let us take what we need for sacrifices and fiery offerings to our God, Adonai," replied Moshe. "We need animals from our herd for sacrificing, but we won't know specifically which animals are needed for Adonai until we get there. So our livestock travels with us — not a hoof stays behind!"

Adonai caused Par'oh's heart to harden again, and he refused to agree.

"Get away from me!" he shouted. "I warn you not to come near me again, Moshe! The day you see my face again is the day you die!"

"You're right," said Moshe ominously. "I will never see your face again."

11:1-3

Just then, Adonai's Presence came to Moshe.

There is one final plague to bring upon Par'oh and Mitzra'im before he lets you go, and
when he sends you away, he will expel you forcefully.

Speak to the people. Have every man and woman request of their Mitzra'imite neighbors
silver, jewels, and gold.

Adonai had caused Benay Yisra'el to be seen favorably by the people of Mitzra'im, and Moshe was held in very high esteem by Par'oh's court and by the people.

When Adonai's Presence left him, Moshe made a final announcement to Par'oh. "These are Adonai's words: 'At midnight, I will go out into Mitzra'im, and all the first-born will die — from Par'oh's own prince who sits on the throne to an ordinary miller's son, and even the first-born of your livestock! Wailing will be heard across all of Mitzra'im such as you have never heard before or will ever hear again! But Benay Yisra'el will not even be nipped by a dog — neither their people or their livestock — so that you will know that Adonai has set them apart from the Mitzra'imites!'"

Moshe indicated Par'oh's courtiers with a sweep of his hand. "'And all these servants will come down to Me and bow low before Me, and ask Me to leave along with all the people who follow Me! Only then will I leave!'"

Moshe departed from Par'oh in fury.

Adonai had told Moshe that it was necessary to demonstrate God's wondrous power, so this was why Par'oh wouldn't listen to him. So while Moshe and Aharon demonstrated God's power for Par'oh, Adonai caused Par'oh's heart to harden so he wouldn't send Benay Yisra'el away.

THE FIRST PESA<u>H</u>

12: 1-6
The Maftir for Shabbat Ha-<u>H</u>odesh starts here.

Verses 1-20 of chapter 12 are read as the special Maftir for Shabbat Ha-<u>H</u>odesh, which is the Shabbat before Rosh <u>H</u>odesh Nisan. Why do you think this is done two weeks before Pesa<u>h</u>? Discuss your ideas.

First Month: In Ye Olden Dayes, the Hebrew months didn't have proper names like they do today. They were simply numbered off or associated with the seasons: First Month, Second Month, Spring Month, etc. So which of our current months does the Torah's First Month correspond to? Hint: it <u>isn't</u> Tishrei...

Adonai's first instructions came to Moshe and Aharon while they were in the land of Mitzra'im.

This month shall be the first month of your calendar year. Tell the community of Yisra'el that on the tenth day of this month, the head of each household shall take a lamb. Households that are too small to use a whole lamb may join up with their neighbors until they have enough people to eat the entire lamb. The lamb should be a year-old goat or sheep, and it must completely free of discolorations and deformities. Keep the lamb until the fourteenth day of the month, when the entire community will slaughter its lambs at dusk.

Paint the lamb's blood on the doorposts and lintels of the houses in which the lambs are being eaten. They shall roast the meat and eat it along with **matzah and maror**. Do not eat any of it raw or boiled in water; roast it — the head,

Do you see any connections between this section of Torah and the modern celebration of Pesah? What are the similarities? What are the differences? Discuss your thoughts.

Matzah and Maror: matzah is literally "unleavened bread" (in other words, flatbread that hasn't risen.) Maror is literally "bitter herbs". But since "matzah" and "maror" are well-known types of food in English, I've left the original Hebrew words as is.

Pass you over: in Hebrew this is וּפָסַחְתִּי עֲלֵכֶם. Look familiar...?

legs, guts, everything — and make sure nothing remains by morning. Burn anything left over. When you eat it, be ready to leave at a moment's notice, with your clothes wrapped tightly, your shoes on your feet, and your staff in hand. Eat it quickly, for this will be the night of Adonai's Pesah.

I will move across the land of Mitzra'im and attack every first-born human and animal. I, Adonai, will pass judgment against the gods of Mitzra'im! The blood around your doors will mark your homes. When I attack Mitzra'im and I see the blood, I will **pass you over** so that no plague comes upon you.

This will be a day of remembrance for you. You will commemorate it as a festival to Adonai and celebrate it in every generation for all time. You will remove all **leavened food** from your homes and eat matzah for seven days. Anyone who fails to remove all leavening by the first day will be cut off from Yisra'el. The first and seventh days will be Holy Days for you. Apart from food preparation, you may not engage in any form of manual labor or business activity. You will observe this festival of matzah every year; it is a requirement for all time, for on this very day I brought you out of Mitzra'im.

Remember this: You will eat matzah from the evening of the fourteenth day to the evening of the twenty-first day! No leavened food shall be found in your homes during these seven days. Anyone who eats leavening will be cut off from the community of Yisra'el — foreigners and Yisra'elites alike! Eat nothing leavened. Wherever you are, eat matzah.

Leavened food: the Hebrew alternates between two words for this: חָמֵץ and שְׂאֹר. The most common understanding is that these words refer to yeast, but it isn't as simple as that. There are over 1500 species of yeast. Are <u>all</u> of them outlawed? What about baking soda or baking powder? What about the carbonation that forms when grains get wet? The customs and requirements associated with Pesah and leavening are very complex. Your rabbi / teacher can help you to navigate them.

12:21-28

When God's Presence left, Moshe immediately summoned the elders of Yisra'el. "Tell each household to slaughter a lamb for the Pesah feast," he instructed. "Dip a bundle of **hyssop** in the lamb's blood and use it to smear the blood on the doorposts and lintels of every home. And make sure no-one leaves the house until morning! Adonai is going to move through Mitzra'im and attack them with a plague. The blood around the doorway will alert Adonai's Messenger of Death to pass over your homes. You must observe this every year — it's a requirement for all time. You'll keep this observance when you finally arrive in the land which Adonai has given to you. **In the future, when your children ask you what this observance means to you**, this is what you should tell them: '**This is the feast of Adonai's Pesah**. It commemorates the moment when God attacked the Mitzra'imites but passed over the homes of Benay Yisra'el in Mitzra'im, and saved us.'"

Hyssop: this is a type of herb that was used for cooking, and medicinal and religious purposes. Apparently, it also made a good paintbrush. ☺

In the future...: here's what verse 26 looks like in Hebrew:
וְהָיָה כִּי־יֹאמְרוּ אֲלֵיכֶם בְּנֵיכֶם מָה הָעֲבֹדָה הַזֹּאת לָכֶם.
This is a famous quote that's used by a child in a famous Pesah guide book. Your teacher / rabbi can help you find it!

This is the feast...: This is another famous passage from the same guidebook. It was used nearly two thousand years ago by a famous rabbi named Gamliel to teach an important lesson, and we've been reteaching the lesson every year since. Flip through the guidebook and see how many other famous lines from *parashat Bo* you can find. Hint: you might need to see them both in Hebrew.

The people lowered their heads and bowed low to the ground. Benay Yisra'el did what Adonai commanded through Moshe and Aharon.

12:29-33

At midnight, Adonai attacked the first-born in Mitzra'im, from Par'oh's first-born to the first-born in the dungeon, as well as the first-born of all the cattle. Par'oh woke up in the middle of the night, along with his servants and everyone in Mitzra'im, and wailing cries were heard everywhere. There wasn't a single home in Mitzra'im where someone wasn't dead.

Par'oh summoned Moshe and Aharon that night. "Get up and get away from my people, you and Benay Yisra'el!" cried Par'oh. "Go and worship Adonai as you said! Take your flocks and herds go... And bless me, as well."

The Mitzra'imites pressed Benay Yisra'el to leave as soon as possible. "If they don't leave, we're all dead!" said the Mitzra'imites to each other.

12: 34-39

The Yisra'elites' baking bowls were packed away with their clothes, so they grabbed their bread dough before it could rise. Then they did as Moshe said, and asked their Mitzra'imite neighbors for jewels, gold, silver, precious items, and clothing. Adonai caused Benay Yisra'el to be viewed favorably by the Mitzra'imites, so they gave them what they asked. In this way, **they stripped Mitzra'im of its wealth.**

Benay Yisra'el set out from Ra'meses to Sukot. They numbered **600,000 marching men**, plus children. Along with their cattle, herds and livestock, a large, mixed group of non-Yisra'elites went with them. Because the Mitzra'imites had tossed them out, there wasn't time to wait to let any dough rise or even to pack food for the journey, and since the dough hadn't risen, they were able to bake it quickly.

There's another famous quote used by Rabban Gamliel somewhere in verses 34-39. See if you can find it! Hint: you may need to see it in Hebrew. Your teacher / rabbi can help you find it.

600,000 marching men: when you take this number, plus the children, women, older people, and the mixed group of non-Yisra'elites, you get to an amazingly high number — well over a million people, and possibly as high as 2.5 to 3 million. The movement of such a large number of people in so short a time has no parallel in recorded history, so it probably qualifies as the single greatest miracle to happen to Benay Yisra'el. There are many opinions and thoughts about how literally we should understand this event. For example, the word for "thousand" (אֶלֶף) also refers to a military unit — a company or a platoon (which connects nicely to the other military terms used in this section of Torah). So did 600 thousand *men* leave all in one night, or did 600 military *units* leave all in one night? The Hebrew supports both ideas — and many other ideas, too! Your teacher / rabbi can help you research this.

They stripped Mitzra'im...: Many people over the centuries have wondered about this comment from verse 36. Does this mean that Benay Yisra'el stole all of Egypt's wealth? The Hebrew in verse 35 reads:

וַיִּשְׁאֲלוּ מִמִּצְרַיִם כְּלֵי־כֶסֶף וּכְלֵי זָהָב וּשְׂמָלֹת...

Literally: "[Benay Yisra'el] asked / begged / requested / borrowed items of silver, items of gold, and clothes from the Mitzra'imites." So which is it? Did Benay Yisra'el *ask* the Mitzra'imites politely for their stuff? Did they *demand* it? Were they *asking* to *borrow* it? The verb וַיִּשְׁאֲלוּ can mean all of these things. Which do you think makes the most sense? Discuss your ideas.

Benay Yisra'el remained in Mitzra'im for a total of 430 years. At the very end of the 430th year, Adonai's entire **congregation** left the land of Mitzra'im. For them, it was a night of vigilance for Adonai, just as it became a night of vigilance for Benay Yisra'el in every generation since.

Congregation: the Torah uses the word צִבְאוֹת י-ה-ו-ה — literally, "Adonai's armies". Why do you think the Torah would describe Benay Yisra'el in this way? Why do you think I chose to translate it as "congregation" instead of "armies"? Think about what you've learned about Benay Yisra'el, and about what happens to them when they reach the Promised Land. Which translation do you think is more appropriate? Discuss your ideas.

Adonai's Presence came to Moshe and Aharon.

These are the rules that relate to the Pesah. No foreigner shall eat from it. However, people who have been bought as slaves and who have been circumcised will eat from it. Your salaried workers and travelers who are staying with you may not eat from it. The Pesah offering must be eaten in one house. You shall not carry the meat outside, nor shall you break the bones. The entire community of Yisra'el must do this!

If a nonresident who lives with you chooses to observe the Pesah to Adonai, he and every male with him must be circumcised. Only then may he approach Adonai to observe the Pesah. He will be considered as if he had been born in Yisra'el. No uncircumcised person may eat from it! Native Yisra'elites and nonresidents will be governed by one set of rules.

All of Benay Yisra'el did as Adonai commanded Moshe and Aharon. This was the very day that Adonai brought Benay Yisra'el out of Mitzra'im in **marching lines**.

Marching lines: This seems like an odd way to describe their departure from Mitzra'im. How does this connect to ideas you may have discussed earlier?

REDEEMING THE FIRST-BORN

13: 1-7

Adonai's Presence came to Moshe again.

The first to come out of any womb, whether human or animal, are holy to Me.

Moshe addressed the people. "Remember this day, for today Adonai has brought you out of the land of Mitzra'im — a land of slavery! — with a mighty hand! Do not eat any leavened bread. Today, you go out during the Spring Month. When Adonai brings you to the land of the Cana'anites, Hitites, Emorites, Hivites, Yevusites — the very land that God promised your ancestors to give to you, a land overflowing with milk and honey — you will maintain this observance in this month. You will eat matzah for seven days, and the seventh day will be a festival to Adonai. Not only will you eat matzah for seven days, but leavened bread shouldn't even be seen with you! No leavening ingredient should be seen with you anywhere within your borders."

13: 8-10

Moshe paused before continuing. "And when you tell your children about today, say to them: 'I do these things because of what Adonai did for me when I left Mitzra'im.' You will make this into a **sign on your hand and a memorial between your eyes** so that Adonai's lessons will always be in the things you say. Adonai brought you out of Mitzra'im with a strong hand, so observe these requirements in their proper time every year."

There's another quote in here that was used famously by... you guessed it: Rabban Gamliel! See if you can find it.

Sign on your hand...memorial...: this should probably look familiar, too. Which ritual items are referred to here? Hint: they're worn by many people during weekday morning services.

Moshe took a breath and went on. "When Adonai brings you to the land God promised your ancestors to give to you, but which is now Cana'anite territory, you will **reserve all first-born human beings and animals for Adonai's service.** These first-borns can be bought back. For example, the cost of buying back a first-born donkey is one sheep. But if you choose not to buy back a first-born animal, you must break its neck. First-born human children may be bought back, as well."

Reserve all first-born...: the Torah includes many customs that seem very strange by our standards, and this is one of them. The basic idea is that all first-born people and animals belong to God. It's kind of like a government tax. But giving up the first-born of every animal in your herd — not to mention your oldest child — can be expensive and heart-wrenching. So the Torah has created a "buy-back" option that enables the tax to be paid to God (or the *kohanim*) while allowing families (and property) to stay together. This *mitzvah* morphed into a ritual called *Pidyon Ha-Ben*, where parents donate a silver shekel (or its equivalent) to "buy back" their first-born baby boys from a descendant of the *kohanim*. This is still done today by many families. Your teacher / rabbi can help you find out more.

But why should the first-born be given to God at all, you ask? For an answer, keep reading Moshe's speech.

There's another question here from another famous child from that famous Pesah guidebook. See if you can find it! Hint: check out verse 14 in the Hebrew.

Moshe explained further. "Going forward, when your children ask you what this is about, tell them how Adonai brought us out of Mitzra'im, from a house of slavery. Tell them that when Par'oh made it nearly impossible for us to go that Adonai killed all the first-born male humans and animals in Mitzra'im. We therefore offer up the first males of our own wombs, which we can buy back."

Moshe finished his speech. "This is what you should put on the sign on your hand and the symbol between your eyes. Adonai brought us out of Mitzra'im with a strong hand."

By now you've probably noticed that the Pesa<u>h</u> *Hagadah* lifts a lot of content from this parashah. Review the various quotes you found. What do they all have in common? Why did Rabban Gamliel choose these particular passages? What is he trying to teach us, and what are we teaching ourselves by repeating them every year?

The *Hagadah* may be the earliest example of what educators call "intergenerational learning". What do you think this means? Why might this be an effective form of education? Explore the connections between your ideas and *parashat Bo*.

Up next...

Be-Shalah! Par'oh has one last change of heart about the departure of his slaves, so he sends his army to bring Yisra'el back to Mitzra'im. But God has one last miracle in store for everyone as Benay Yisra'el prepare to cross a very famous body of water. Moshe and his sister, Miryam, lead Benay Yisra'el in singing a couple of victory songs before they head off into the wilderness. *Parashat Be-Shalah* also includes some famous incidents involving food from heaven and warfare with Yisra'el's archenemy...

TORAH AND BLESSINGS IN HEBREW
SHEMOT / EXODUS 10: 1-11

Before the Torah reading, recite one of the following blessings.
Your rabbi or teacher will tell you which one is appropriate for your community.

You call out:	**You call out:**
בָּרְכוּ אֶת יְיָ הַמְבֹרָךְ.	בָּרְכוּ אֶת יְיָ הַמְבֹרָךְ.
The congregation responds:	**The congregation responds:**
בָּרוּךְ יְיָ הַמְבֹרָךְ לְעוֹלָם וָעֶד.	בָּרוּךְ יְיָ הַמְבֹרָךְ לְעוֹלָם וָעֶד.
You say it back to them:	**You say it back to them:**
בָּרוּךְ יְיָ הַמְבֹרָךְ לְעוֹלָם וָעֶד.	בָּרוּךְ יְיָ הַמְבֹרָךְ לְעוֹלָם וָעֶד.
You continue:	**You continue:**
בָּרוּךְ אַתָּה יְיָ אֱלֹהֵינוּ מֶלֶךְ הָעוֹלָם, אֲשֶׁר קֵרְבָנוּ לַעֲבוֹדָתוֹ וְנָתַן לָנוּ אֶת תּוֹרָתוֹ. בָּרוּךְ אַתָּה יְיָ, נוֹתֵן הַתּוֹרָה.	בָּרוּךְ אַתָּה יְיָ אֱלֹהֵינוּ מֶלֶךְ הָעוֹלָם, אֲשֶׁר בָּחַר בָּנוּ מִכָּל הָעַמִּים וְנָתַן לָנוּ אֶת תּוֹרָתוֹ. בָּרוּךְ אַתָּה יְיָ, נוֹתֵן הַתּוֹרָה.
Let us praise Adonai, the Blessed One!	Let us praise Adonai, the Blessed One!
Let Adonai, the Blessed One, be praised forever!	Let Adonai, the Blessed One, be praised forever!
We praise You, Adonai our God, Ruler of the universe, Who drew us close to God's Work and gave us God's Torah.	We praise You, Adonai our God, Ruler of the universe, Who chose us from all the nations to be given God's Torah.
We praise You, Adonai, the Giver of Torah.	We praise You, Adonai, the Giver of Torah.

השׂערה אביב והפשתה גבעל והזזטה

והכסמת לא נכו כי אפילת הנה ויצא

משה מעם פרעה את העיר ויפרש כפיו

אל יהוה ויחדלו הקלות והברד ומטר

לא נתך ארצה וירא פרעה כי זדל

המטר והברד והקלת ויסף לזזטא

ויכבד לבו הוא ועבדיו ויזזק לב פרעה

ולא שלח את בני ישראל כאשׁר דבר

יהוה ביד משה

ויאמר יהוה אל משׂ בא אל פרעה כי

אני הכבדתי את לבו ואת לב עבדיו

למען שתי אתתי אלה בקרבו ולמען

תספר באזני בנך ובן בנך את אשר

התעללתי במצרים ואת אתתי אשׁר

שמתי בם וידעתם כי אני יהוה ויבא

משה ואהרן אל פרעה ויאמרו אליו כה

אמר יהוה אלהי העברים עד מתי

מאנת לענת מפני שלח עמי

ויעבדני כי אם מאן אתה לשלח את

עמי הנני מביא מזזר ארבה

בגבלך וכסה את עין הארץ ולא יוכל

לראת את הארץ ואכל את יתר

הפלטה הנשארת לכם מן הברד ואכל

את כל העץ הצמזז לכם מן

השדה ומלאו בתיך ובתי כל עבדיך

ובתי כל מצרים אשר לא ראו אבתיך

ואבות אבתיך מיום היותם על האדמה

עד היום הזה ויפן ויצא מעם

28

עליה ב'	עליה א'
4. כִּי	1. וַיֹּאמֶר יְהוָֹה אֶל־מֹשֶׁה
אִם־מָאֵן אַתָּה לְשַׁלֵּחַ אֶת־עַמִּי	בֹּא אֶל־פַּרְעֹה
הִנְנִי מֵבִיא מָחָר	כִּי־אֲנִי
אַרְבֶּה בִּגְבֻלֶךָ:	הִכְבַּדְתִּי אֶת־לִבּוֹ וְאֶת־לֵב עֲבָדָיו
	לְמַעַן
5. וְכִסָּה אֶת־עֵין הָאָרֶץ	שִׁתִי
וְלֹא יוּכַל לִרְאֹת אֶת־הָאָרֶץ	אֹתֹתַי אֵלֶּה בְּקִרְבּוֹ:
וְאָכַל ׀ אֶת־יֶתֶר הַפְּלֵטָה	
הַנִּשְׁאֶרֶת לָכֶם מִן־הַבָּרָד	2. וּלְמַעַן
וְאָכַל אֶת־כָּל־הָעֵץ	תְּסַפֵּר בְּאָזְנֵי בִנְךָ וּבֶן־בִּנְךָ
הַצֹּמֵחַ לָכֶם מִן־הַשָּׂדֶה:	אֵת אֲשֶׁר הִתְעַלַּלְתִּי בְּמִצְרַיִם
	וְאֶת־אֹתֹתַי אֲשֶׁר־שַׂמְתִּי בָם
6. וּמָלְאוּ בָתֶּיךָ	וִידַעְתֶּם כִּי־אֲנִי יְהוָה:
וּבָתֵּי כָל־עֲבָדֶיךָ וּבָתֵּי כָל־מִצְרַיִם	
אֲשֶׁר לֹא־רָאוּ אֲבֹתֶיךָ	3. וַיָּבֹא מֹשֶׁה וְאַהֲרֹן אֶל־פַּרְעֹה
וַאֲבוֹת אֲבֹתֶיךָ	וַיֹּאמְרוּ אֵלָיו
מִיּוֹם	כֹּה־אָמַר יְהוָֹה אֱלֹהֵי הָעִבְרִים
הֱיוֹתָם עַל־הָאֲדָמָה	עַד־מָתַי מֵאַנְתָּ
עַד הַיּוֹם הַזֶּה	לֵעָנֹת מִפָּנָי
וַיִּפֶן וַיֵּצֵא מֵעִם פַּרְעֹה:	שַׁלַּח עַמִּי וְיַעַבְדֻנִי:

פרעה ויאמרו עבדי פרעה אליו עד מתי
יהיה זה לנו למוקש שלח את האנשים
ויעבדו את יהוה אלהיהם הטרם תדע כי
אבדה מצרים ויושב את משה ואת
אהרן אל פרעה ויאמר אלהם לכו עבדו
את יהוה אלהיכם מי ומי
ההלכים ויאמר משה בנערינו ובזקנינו
נלך בבנינו ובבנותינו בצאננו ובבקרנו
נלך כי חג יהוה לנו ויאמר אלהם יהי כן
יהוה עמכם כאשר אשלח אתכם ואת
טפכם ראו כי רעה נגד פניכם לא כן
לכו נא הגברים ועבדו את יהוה כי אתה
אתם מבקשים ויגרש אתם מאת פני
פרעה ויאמר יהוה אל
משה נטה ידך על ארץ מצרים בארבה
ויעל על ארץ מצרים ויאכל את כל
עשב הארץ את כל אשר השאיר
הברד ויט משה את מטהו על ארץ
מצרים ויהוה נהג רוח קדים בארץ כל
היום ההוא וכל הלילה הבקר היה ורוח
הקדים נשא את הארבה ויעל הארבה
על כל ארץ מצרים וינח בכל גבול
מצרים כבד מאד לפניו לא היה כן
ארבה כמהו ואחריו לא יהיה כן

10. וַיֹּאמֶר אֲלֵהֶם

יְהִי כֵן יהוה עִמָּכֶם

כַּאֲשֶׁר

אֲשַׁלַּח אֶתְכֶם וְאֶת־טַפְּכֶם

רְאוּ

כִּי רָעָה נֶגֶד פְּנֵיכֶם:

11. לֹא כֵן

לְכוּ־נָא הַגְּבָרִים

וְעִבְדוּ אֶת־יהוֹה

כִּי אֹתָהּ אַתֶּם מְבַקְשִׁים

וַיְגָרֶשׁ אֹתָם

מֵאֵת פְּנֵי פַרְעֹה:

8. וַיּוּשַׁ֗ב

אֶת־מֹשֶׁ֤ה וְאֶֽת־אַהֲרֹן֙ אֶל־פַּרְעֹ֔ה

וַיֹּ֣אמֶר אֲלֵהֶ֔ם

לְכ֥וּ עִבְד֖וּ אֶת־יְהֹוָ֣ה אֱלֹהֵיכֶ֑ם

מִ֥י וָמִ֖י הַהֹלְכִֽים׃

9. וַיֹּ֣אמֶר מֹשֶׁ֔ה

בִּנְעָרֵ֤ינוּ וּבִזְקֵנֵ֙ינוּ֙ נֵלֵ֔ךְ

בְּבָנֵ֥ינוּ וּבִבְנוֹתֵ֛נוּ

בְּצֹאנֵ֥נוּ וּבִבְקָרֵ֖נוּ נֵלֵ֑ךְ

כִּ֥י חַג־יְהֹוָ֖ה לָֽנוּ׃

7. וַיֹּאמְרוּ֩ עַבְדֵ֨י פַרְעֹ֜ה אֵלָ֗יו

עַד־מָתַי֙

יִהְיֶ֨ה זֶ֥ה לָ֙נוּ֙ לְמוֹקֵ֔שׁ

שַׁלַּח֙ אֶת־הָ֣אֲנָשִׁ֔ים

וְיַֽעַבְד֖וּ אֶת־יְהֹוָ֣ה אֱלֹהֵיהֶ֑ם

הֲטֶ֣רֶם תֵּדַ֔ע

כִּ֥י אָבְדָ֖ה מִצְרָֽיִם׃

After the Torah reading, recite the following blessing.

בָּרוּךְ אַתָּה יְיָ אֱלֹהֵינוּ מֶלֶךְ הָעוֹלָם, אֲשֶׁר נָתַן לָנוּ תּוֹרַת אֱמֶת,

וְחַיֵּי עוֹלָם נָטַע בְּתוֹכֵנוּ. בָּרוּךְ אַתָּה יְיָ, נוֹתֵן הַתּוֹרָה.

We praise You, Adonai our God, Ruler of the universe,
Who planted eternal life among us by giving us a Teaching of truth.

We praise You, Adonai, the Giver of Torah.

TA'AMEI HA-MIKRA: TROP CHARTS

Let's face it: learning trop can be very difficult. Most of us are used to the idea that each musical sign represents a single tone, but with trop, most signs (*ta'amim*) represent musical phrases. To add to the difficulty, there are 28 separate trop signs — each with a unique musical phrase, and sometimes the phrasing changes depending on the combination of *ta'amim* (though very few readings contain all 28 *ta'amim*). Sure, you can find sheet music to help you out, but if you're like me and don't read music, you might wind up more confused. Oy!

I developed the charts in this section to help people like me. Most of the *ta'amim* are grouped into sequences that are used commonly in the Tanah. The grids enable the teacher and the student to chart the music as it goes higher or lower.

These charts have proven quite helpful with my own students. I hope you find them just as useful!

אֶתְנַחְתָּא

Etnahta divides a verse into two broad ideas. Tipha, Zakef, Segol, and Shalshelet then divide Etnahta into smaller ideas. Etnahta always comes after Tiphah.

Common Patterns

מֵירְכָא טִפְחָא מוּנַח אֶתְנַחְתָּא

טִפְחָא מוּנַח אֶתְנַחְתָּא

מֵירְכָא טִפְחָא אֶתְנַחְתָּא

טִפְחָא אֶתְנַחְתָּא

מוּנַח מוּנַח אֶתְנַחְתָּא

What's the point of all this trop?

Apart from musical notations, the trop (or, more properly, *te'amim*) tell us where to put the correct emphasis in each word and sentence. They also function as grammatical and syntactical notations, telling us when to pause in our reading, when to read quickly, etc. So we don't just read the punctuation — we sing it! There are seven distinct vocal systems for chanting the Tanah. Most people are familiar with Torah and Haftarah. See if you can find out what the other five are!

אתנחתא panel

Common Patterns

וַיֹּאמֶר יְהֹוָה אֶל־מֹשֶׁה לֵּאמֹר אֶתְנַחְתָּא

אֶתְנַחְתָּא וַיֹּאמֶר יְהֹוָה אֶל־מֹשֶׁה

אֶתְנַחְתָּא וַיֹּאמֶר יְהֹוָה אֶל־מֹשֶׁה

אֶתְנַחְתָּא וַיֹּאמֶר יְהֹוָה

אֶתְנַחְתָּא וַיֹּאמֶר יְהֹוָה אֶל־מֹשֶׁה

אתנחתא

Etnahta divides a verse into two broad ideas. Tipha, Zakef, Segol, and Shalshelet then divide Etnahta into smaller ideas. Etnahta always comes after Tiphah.

סוף־פסוק panel

Common Patterns

וַיֹּאמֶר מֹשֶׁה אֶל־יְהֹוָה

סוֹף־פָּסוּק וַיֹּאמֶר יְהֹוָה

סוֹף־פָּסוּק וַיֹּאמֶר יְהֹוָה

וַיֹּאמֶר יְהֹוָה אֶל־מֹשֶׁה סוֹף־פָּסוּק

וַיֹּאמֶר יְהֹוָה אֶל־מֹשֶׁה סוֹף־פָּסוּק

סוֹף־פָּסוּק

Sof Pasuk is also called סילוק (Siluk). It marks the end of a verse. Tipha and Zakef subdivide Sof Pasuk into smaller ideas. Sof Pasuk always comes after Tiphah.

TORAH TROP

Common Patterns

זָקֵף קָטֹן

זָקֵף קָטֹן רְבִיעִ֘י אֶתְנַחְתָּ֑א

טִפְּחָ֖א פַּשְׁטָ֙א זָקֵ֔ף

זָקֵ֔ף יְתִ֚יב

יְתִ֚יב זָקֵ֔ף
(see Yetiv card)

זָקֵ֔ף קָטֹן רְבִיעִ֘י
(see Yetiv card)

זָקֵף–גָּדוֹל

Zakef divides Etnahta and Sof Pasuk into smaller ideas, but only if they already have a Tipha, Revi'a, Pashta and Yetiv suubdivide Zakef into even simpler ideas. Zakef-Katon (a.k.a Katon) is more common than Zakef-Gadol.

Common Patterns

טִפְחָ֖ה טֵבִיר֩ וַיֹּ֥אמֶר

טֵבִ֛יר אֶתְנַחְתָּ֑א

גֵּרְשַׁ֞יִם אֱלֹהִ֑ים

טֵבִ֛יר אֱלֹהִ֑ים וַיֹּ֥אמֶר

טֵבִ֛יר אֶתְנַחְתָּ֑א וַיֹּ֥אמֶר

טֵבִ֛יר אֱלֹהִ֑ים

תְּבִיר

When a Tipha idea has three or more words, it needs to be subdivided. We use Tevir for this subdivision.

TORAH TROP

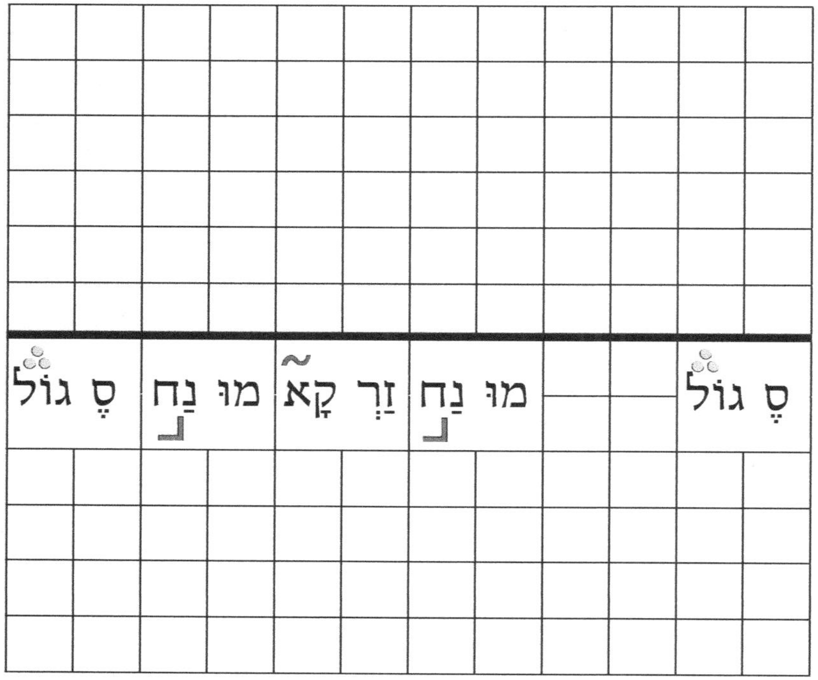

Top section

זָקֵף־גָּדוֹל

Common Patterns

זָקֵף־גָּדוֹל

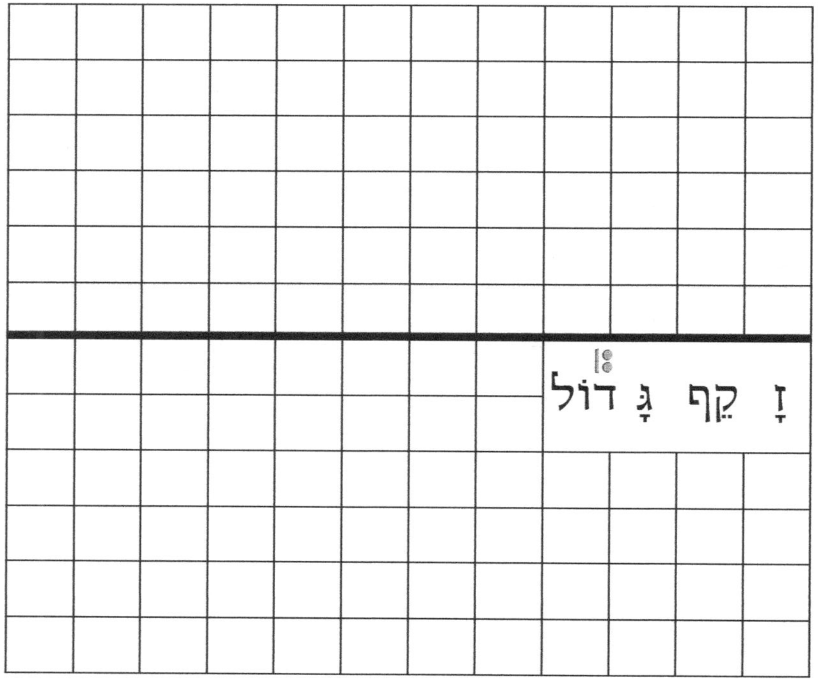

זָקֵף־גָּדוֹל

Zakef divides Etnahta and Sof Pasuk into smaller ideas, but only if they already have a Tipha. Revi'a, Pashta and Yetiv suubdivide Zakef into even simpler ideas. Zakef-Gadol is only found on short words and it never uses a Link.

Bottom section

Common Patterns

סְגוֹל תִּפְחָה
סְגוֹל תִּפְחָה אַקְדֵּי תִּפְחָה
סְגוֹל אַקְדֵּי
סְגוֹל תִּפְחָה אַקְדֵּי תִּפְחָה

סֶגּוֹל

Segol divides Etnahta into smaller ideas, but only if it already has a Tipha and at least one Zakef. Revi'a, Pashta, Yetiv, and Zarka subdivide Segol into simpler ideas. Segol never appears on the first word of a verse.

Common Patterns

רְבִיעַ

מֵרְכָא רְבִיעַ

מֻנַּח רְבִיעַ ׀ לְגַרְמֵהּ

דַּרְגָּא מֻנַּח רְבִיעַ

רְבִיעַ

When Tip<u>h</u>a, Zakef, or Segol need to be subdivided and they have one or two Tevirs, Revi'a is used as the Divider.

Common Patterns

גֵּרֵשׁ

קַדְמָא אַזְלָא
(a.k.a. אַזְלָא גֵּרֵשׁ)

קַדְמָא אַזְלָא גֵּרֵשׁ

תְּלִישָׁא־קְטַנָּה קַדְמָא אַזְלָא גֵּרֵשׁ

גֵּרֵשׁ

If a Tevir, Pashta, Revi'a or Zarka needs to be subdivided, the subdivider is usually Geresh or Gershayim.

TORAH TROP

Common Patterns

פַּשְׁטָ֙א

Pashta is only used on the last or second-last syllable of a word. If a Pashta is needed on the first syllable, we use Yetiv, instead. Yetiv never uses a Link.

Common Patterns

גֵּרְשַׁ֞יִם

If a Tevir, Pashta, Revi'a or Zarka needs to be subdivided, the subdivider is usually Geresh or Gershayim.

37

TORAH TROP

Common Patterns מֵרְכָ֖א פָּזֵ֖ר

פָּזֵ֖ר

Pazer is used to subdivide Tevir, Revi'a, Pashta, and Zarka. Pazer can be linked to up to six Munahs.

Common Patterns תְּלִישָׁה־גְדוֹלָה

תְּלִישָׁה־גְדוֹלָה

When Tevir, Revi'a, Pashta, or Zarka need to be subdivided, Telishah-Gedolah is sometimes used. When the accent is not on the first syllable, a second Telishah-Gedolah is often added to mark the stress. Telishah-Gedolah can be linked to up to six Munahs.

D'VAR TORAH WRITING GUIDE

This guide is intended to give you a general idea of what a typical D'var Torah looks like. Yours may not look exactly like this — it will, of course, be written by you and not me! — but it should include all of these elements. As always, make sure you consult with your rabbi / teacher.

1. Don't thank people for coming — that's something you can tell your guests at the party afterwards. The person giving the D'var Torah is called a *Darshan* — literally, an "explainer". The congregation will thank *you* for explaining the weekly readings to *them*.

2. In one or two paragraphs, summarize the content of the Torah and Haftarah readings for that day.

3. Quote a verse or idea from the Torah and/or Haftarah in Hebrew and in English, and discuss its relevance in our times. This is when you bring in your own commentaries and tell us what you've learned from our ancient and modern teachers.

4. Explain how the idea you've chosen has meaning to you. You can discuss the impact the D'var Torah may have had on how you're going to lead your life, how it's affected your commitment to Judaism and its values, etc.

5. If it fits with your ideas, you may want to talk about your parents, grandparents or other family members and role models and what positive values or lessons you've learned from them. Note: this is not the same as thanking them. Save the "thank you's" for after the service!

6. Final thoughts: what does becoming a Bar/Bat Mitzvah mean to you? Why is it special to you and what have you learned in the process of studying for today? Typically, this is where you bring your discussion back to the original idea you chose from the Torah / Haftarah.

7. Your D'var Torah should be no more than four or five double-spaced pages — roughly the length of a five to seven minute speech.

My **parashah**, book from the Torah, and chapter/verse

My **Haftarah** book and chapter/verse reference...

What the HAFTARAH says in my own words:

What the TORAH says in my own words:

Questions I have about my TORAH reading, Haftarah, Bar/Bat Mitzvah process, or Judaism in general (minimum 3):	Questions my parents have about my TORAH reading, Haftarah, Bar/Bat Mitzvah process, or Judaism in general (minimum 3):

SECTIONS OF TORAH THAT STAND OUT FOR ME...

Chapter : Verse OR Section	What it says in my own words	Why it stands out for me

SECTIONS OF HAFTARAH THAT STAND OUT FOR ME...

Chapter : Verse OR Section	What it says in my own words	Why it stands out for me

One idea or theme I want to talk about (based on my choices from charts 3 and 4):	
Verse or section from the Torah or Haftarah that relates to my theme (choose 1 or 2 from charts 3 and/or 4 and write them here):	

Commentator	The commentator's own words	What I think the commentator is trying to teach
	→	→
	→	→
	→	→

One idea or theme I want to talk about: (copy from previous chart)	
Verse or section from the Torah or Haftarah that relates to my theme: (copy from previous chart)	

Commentator (copy from previous chart)	**What I think the commentator is trying to teach** (copy from previous chart)	**How this teaching relates to my life or the world around me**
↑	↑	
↑	↑	
↑	↑	

One idea or theme I want to talk about:

(copy from previous chart)

Verse or section from the Torah or Haftarah that relates to my theme:

(copy from previous chart)

Commentator

(copy from previous chart)

How this teaching relates to my life or the world around me

(copy from previous chart)

My lesson for this parashah (bring all your ideas together)

INCREDIBLY HANDY TIME LINE

The dates here are approximate. The two main columns compare the Tanah's chronology with samples of writings from ancient Yisra'el's neighbors that relate to events in the Tanah. There are also thousands of Hebrew inscriptions and documents dug up by archeologists, but unfortunately I don't have space to mention them all! The narrow column on the left shows you when the books of the Torah and *Nevi'im* (Prophets) <u>take place</u>, **not** <u>when they were written</u>. See if you can locate your own Torah / Haftarah readings on this time line!

WHEN TORAH BOOKS TAKE PLACE	TIME LINE FROM THE TANAH (TORAH & PROPHETS ONLY)		STUFF WRITTEN ABOUT YISRA'EL BY YISRA'EL'S NEIGHBORS
BERESHIT	First Jewish family: Avraham, Sarah, Yitzhak, Rivkah, Ya'akov, Le'ah, Rahel, Yosef and all his brothers	**1600 BCE** 3600 years ago	
		1500 BCE 3500 years ago	
	Benay Yisra'el in Mitzra'im	**1400 BCE** 3400 years ago	
		1300 BCE 3300 years ago	
SHEMOT, VAYIKRA, BAMIDBAR, DEVARIM	Time of Moshe and the Exodus	**1200 BCE** 3200 years ago	Egyptian Pharaoh Merneptah records a list of nations living in Cana'an. "Yisra'el" is included in the list (1205 BCE)
	Benay Yisra'el capture land of Yisra'el		

When Navi Books Take Place			
Yehoshu'a, Shoftim	Benay Yisra'el in Mitzra'im Time of Moshe and the Exodus Benay Yisra'el capture the land of Yisra'el and settle it. Time of the *Shoftim* (tribal chiefs).	**1200 BCE** 3200 years ago **1100 BCE** 3100 years ago	Egyptian Pharaoh Merneptah records a list of nations living in Cana'an. "Yisra'el" is included in the list (1205 BCE)
Shemu'el	Time of King Sha'ul, King David and King Shlomo; First Temple is built; Kingdom of Yisra'el established	**1000 BCE** 3000 years ago	
1 Melahim	Kingdom splits into Yehudah and Yisra'el (922 BCE) Book of *1 Melahim* describes invasion of Yehudah by Pharaoh Shishak	**900 BCE** 2900 years ago	Egyptian Pharaoh Shishak writes a victory monument about invading the region in and around Yisra'el
2 Melahim, Amos, Hoshe'a, Nahum, Micah, Yish'ayah #1	Time of Eliyahu and Elisha; Book of *2 Melahim* describes a rebellion against Yisra'el by Mesha, king of Mo'ab; *2 Melahim* also describes war between Aram, Yehudah, and Yisra'el	**800 BCE** 2800 years ago	King Mesha of Mo'ab makes a stone monument describing his rebellion against Israel; Anonymous king of Aram makes a stone monument describing war with Yehudah & Yisra'el
	Ashur conquers Yisra'el (722-720 BCE) Books of *2 Melahim* and *Yish'ayah* describe Assyrian invasions of Yehudah and Yisra'el	**700 BCE** 2700 years ago	Assyrian kings Tiglath-Pileser III and Shalmaneser V write inscriptions and wall carvings about conquering Israel; Assyrian king Sennacherib writes inscription about his invasion of Yehudah
2 Melahim, Tzefanyah, Yirmiyah, Yehezk'el, Yish'ayah #2, Ovadyah	**Bavel conquers Yehudah (590's-586 BCE)** Yerushalayim destroyed (586 BCE)	**600 BCE** 2600 years ago	**Babylonians write inscriptions about their invasion and conquest of Yehudah**
Hagai, Zeharyah, Habakuk, Mal'ahi	Cyrus of Persia allows exiles to return from Bavel; Temple rebuilt; time of Nehemiyah & Ezra	**500 BCE** 2500 years ago	Persia conquers Babylon; Persian King Cyrus II writes inscription about his policy of allowing all exiled people to return home

WHEN *NAVI* BOOKS TAKE PLACE				
HAGAI, ZEHARYAH, HABAKUK, MAL'AHI	Cyrus of Persia allows exiles to return from Bavel; Temple rebuilt; time of Nehemiyah & Ezra		**500 BCE** 2500 years ago	Persia conquers Babylon; Persian King Cyrus II writes inscription about his policy of allowing all exiled people to return home
			400 BCE 2400 years ago	
		Books of the Torah, Prophets, and other pieces of literature are edited and compiled into the Tanah	**300 BCE** 2300 years ago	Greek Empire defeats Persia and takes control of the land of Israel
		Jews successfully rebel against Greek Seleucid Empire & establish kingdom of Judea (Hanukah)	**200 BCE** 2200 years ago	
	Time of the Mishnah (final compilation roughly 200 CE)		**100 BCE** 2100 years ago	Dead Sea Scrolls are written and hidden in caves in the Judean Desert · Roman Empire takes control of Judea
		Jews rebel against Rome; Jerusalem and the Temple are destroyed (70 CE)	**1 BCE / 1 CE** 2000 years ago	**Romans build a massive arch with carvings that depict the victory over the Jews**
			200 CE 1800 years ago	

Ease your way into learning the Trop for Torah and Haftarah!

Our Trop Flashcards enhance any Bar/Bat Mitzvah study program. 28 5"x7" flashcards feature:

- the position of each ta'am in a word
- explanations that let you know what each ta'am is used for
- the most common patterns for each ta'am
- handy music charts
- a color-coding system to help students visualize the music
- suggestions for use
- terribly convenient explanatory notes and charts

Each set also includes a 12-page booklet that explains how the Trop system works.

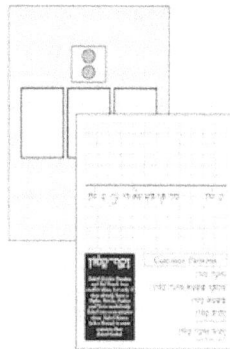

Zakef-Katon card, Do-It-Yourself edition (front and back sides).

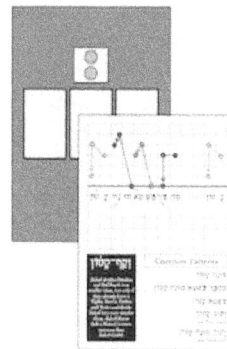

Zakef-Katon card, Haftarah edition (front and back sides).

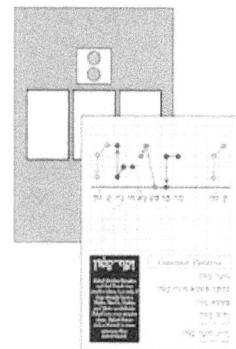

Zakef-Katon card, Torah edition (front and back sides).

Trop Poster Set

Excellent companion for teaching Trop to groups of any size!

Use the posters on their own or with our Trop Flashcards, Bar/Bat Mitzvah Survival Guides, or Ultimate Torah Trainer!

Disjunctive Ta'amim: Dividers and their Levels

Contains 3 12"x18" posters:

- the Disjunctive ta'amim and when they're used
- the Conjunctive ta'amim and when they're used
- how ta'amim are used to divide a verse into segments

Simple explanations and examples!

The set also includes this handy explanation booklet!

Practical Solutions for Jewish Education
www.adventurejudaism.net

Made in Canada.
www.adventurejudaism.net
© 2015 Adventure Judaism Classroom Solutions

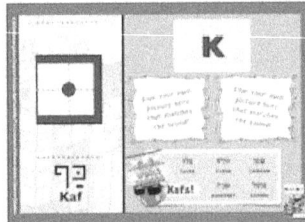

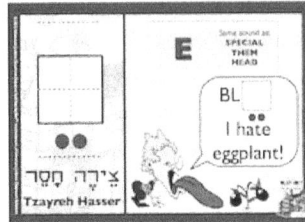

A fun way to learn about the Holy Days and the order of the Hebrew months!

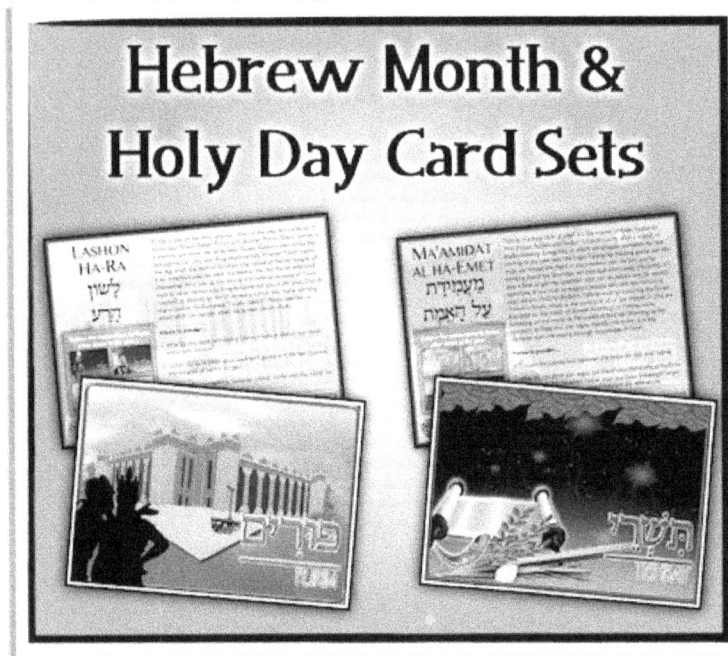

The Hebrew months and Holy Days come alive with the Hagim & Hodashim Cards series. Meet any classroom or programming need with our large display cards, flashcards for small groups, or playing cards for active learning through games. Use them for:

✓ Learning the order of the Hebrew months and Holy Days

✓ Connecting months and events inthe year to Jewish values

✓ Designing a values-based program for the year

✓ And more!

Hebrew Month & Holy Day Card Sets

LASHON HA-RA
לשון הרע

MA'AMIDAT AL HA-EMET
מעמידת על האמת

פורים
YOM HA-ATZMAUT
יום העצמאות

11"x8" Display Cards

AHAVAT ZION
אהבת ציון

The new year for trees and plants.

7"x5" Flashcards

שבט

4"x3" Playing Cards

The start of the Jewish year

1st month of the Jewish year

The 11"x8" display cards are perfect for word walls, sorting games, class displays, and more.

The 7"x5" flashcards are great for working with small groups.

The 4"x3" playing cards are great for match games, fish, memory games, and more. Suggestions for games are included.

www.ingramcontent.com/pod-product-compliance
Lightning Source LLC
Chambersburg PA
CBHW081230020426
42331CB00012B/3112